Fujifilm Instax Mini 9 Instant Camera User Guide

How to use your Fujifilm Instax Mini 9 Instant Camera User Guide like a Pro for Adults/Kids

Gladys E. Young

Contents

INTRODUCTION

If this is your first time to use an instant camera, you might feel somehow nervous when the time comes to load your first pack of film into your Instax mini 9 camera. However from this guide book, you are going to learn how to load and use the Instax mini 9 camera, which includes important shooting tips, that you need to know, if you don't know these things, you may end up wasting a lot of time, money and film trying to figure out and wondering why your pictures are not coming out as it ought to.

You should first take note that your Fujifilm Instax mini camera is an instant film, i.e it shoots instant films, the photo is readily available once it is shot.

When you buy this camera, know that the film does not come along with it, so don't buy it and go home all excited only to find out that there is nothing to shoot with, make sure you also buy along with your camera, a pack of Instax mini 9 film.

If you would be shooting a lot of photos with your camera, you can buy the film in bulk and save some money.

When you buy the mini 9, you will find the following in the box- the camera, a nice wrist strap for the camera, a close-up lens attachment, a super cool sticker and an instruction manual.

I hope you find this guide useful.

CHAPTER ONE: FUJI FILM INSTAX MINI 9, PART NAMES

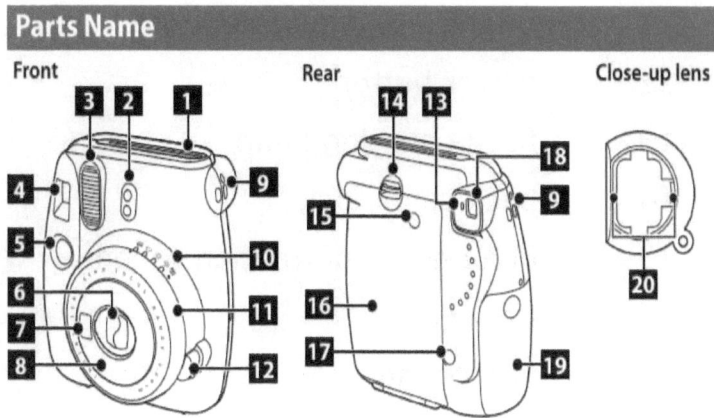

Parts Name

Front   Rear   Close-up lens

The picture above depicts the various parts of the Fujifilm Instax mini 9 camera, the parts are listed below:

1. film ejection slot
2. light sensor
3. flash lampface
4. viewfinder
5. shutter button
6. lens/lens cover

7. self-portrait mirror

8. lens barrel

9. strap hook

10.   brightness indicator

11.   brightness adjustment dial

12.   power button

13.   flash charging lamp

14.   back cover lock

15.   film pack confirmation window

16.   back cover

17.   film counter

18.   eyepiece

19.   battery lid

20.   tabs (back)

HOW TO SET UP THE CAMERA

1. Insert the Batteries

To set up the Instax mini 9 camera, the first step is to insert the batteries, and how to do this is to-open the battery door over- on the side, top it down, then put in the batteries, close the battery door and your camera is now set up.

Next is to turn the camera on, this is very easy, just push the little button by the side of the lens and the lens will pops out- now your camera is on. You can look on top of the lens and when you see an orange e red light on, you know that it is ready for shooting.

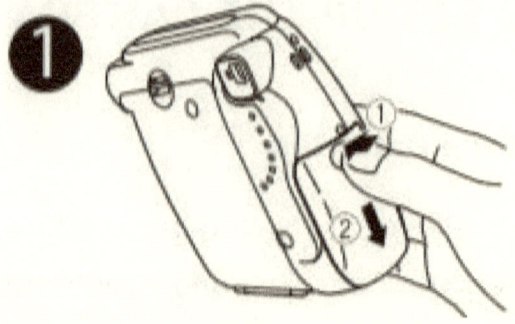

Push up the battery lid lock, then slide off the batter cover.

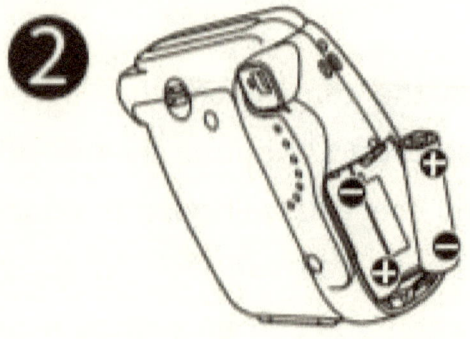

Insert two AA batteries matching the + and – polarities

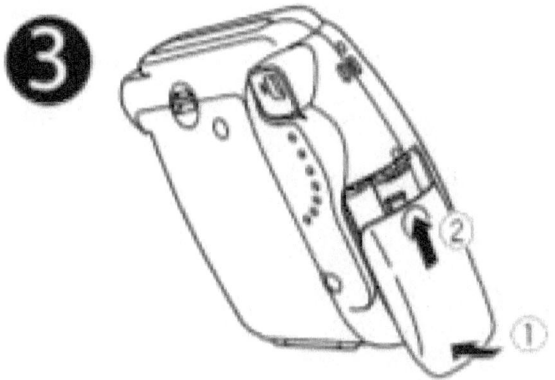

Slide on the battery lid to close

Take Note:

- You should use only new alkaline batteries which are of the same brand/type (AAONLY).
- Only alkaline batteries should be used and no other.
- Both batteries should be replaced in any of the cases listed below:

  When the red lamp on viewfinder lights and

  When no lamp lights or blinks even though the power is turned on

- You should also know that 100 pictures (which is roughly 10packs of INSTAX mini film) can be taken with new alkaline batteries
- Another fact to note is-the battery may perform slowly when it is cold. If that is the case, warm up the batteries to room temperature before using this camera.
- Lastly, use the supplied batteries for validation.

2. How to Load the Instax Mini Film Pack

If you are just starting to use the Instax mini 9, first turn the camera off, then get the film from the box, the film is usually in a sealed pack, you have to tear off the seal, to get the film. Be careful with the film as it is very sensitive, you have to treat it with care, so don't leave it in a hot or harsh environment, and do not allow it get cold as that can totally damage it. Endeavour to leave it in room temperature and don't let it get it wet.

Important: On how to handle the film, once you open the sealed pack, be very careful with it. The reason is because, when you take the film out, you will see that there are some "no finger little pictures" all over it. That is to notify you that you should not squish it, because if you squish it with your finger, know that there are so many chemicals that make the instant film work. So you will totally mess up your photos if you squish it.

Thus, do well to hold your photos from the edges, handle it with care. Now to load the film, check around the back of the camera, you will see a little yellow dot on the top side of the camera where the film will be inserted. And on the left top side of the film you will also see a little yellow dot, line up both yellow dots and drop the film inside, then close the door of the film.

On the door of the film, you will also observe a tiny little window that will help you tell whether or not there is film in the camera. If the colour from the window is yellow, you will know there is film inside the camera, if there is no yellow dot, then know that it's empty.

In your pack of film, there is something called a dark slide- it's like cardboard cover that doesn't let the light damage the film which means the first image you take is not going to be a photo. So don't get everything all set up ready to take a shot, you have to take that dark slide off first.

So, turn on the camera, then press the shutter release and the dark slide will come out. When it comes out, check the slide and you will see written on it **"this is not a film"** so that you won't get confused.

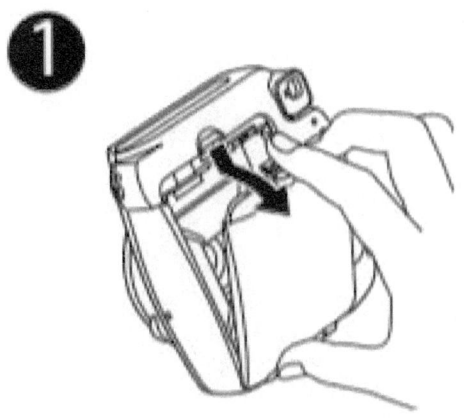

Press down the back cover lock to open the back cover

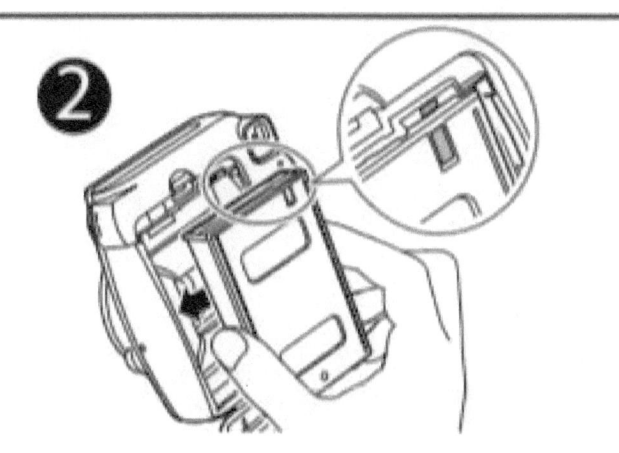

First, hold both sides of the film pack, then align the yellow marks on the camera and the film pack as indicated on the INSTAX mini film pack instructions, then insert it straight.

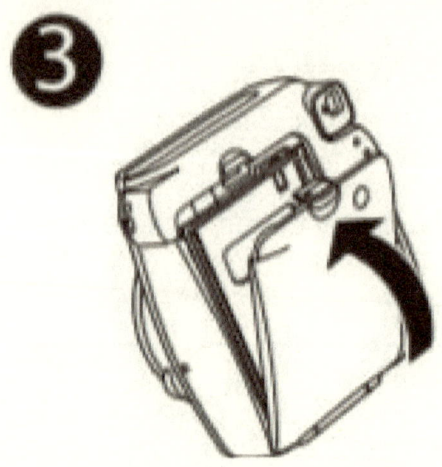

Close the back cover until the back cover lock clicks into place.

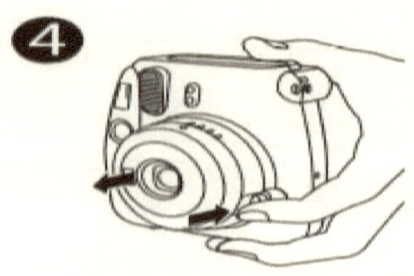

When you turn the camera on (press the power button to put in on) there is a flash charging lamp on the left of the eyepiece that will start blinking, (this indicates that the flash is charging).

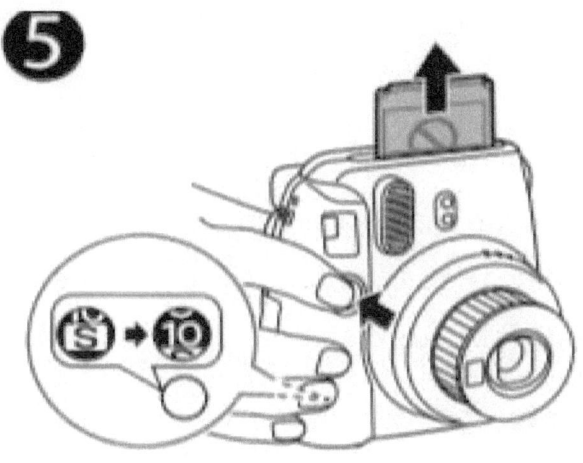

When you press the shutter button, the film cover, (black) is ejected, and the film counter display on the back changes from "S' TO "10"

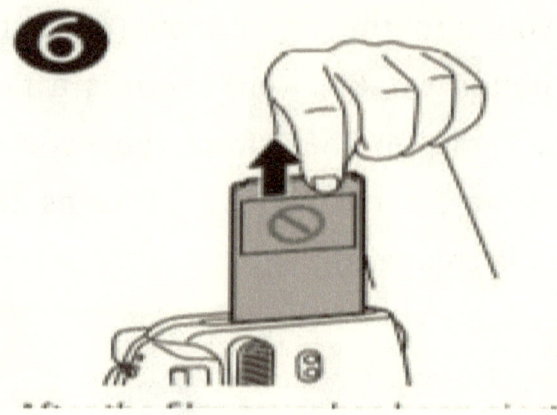

After the film cover has been ejected (the camera stops making sound), hold the edge of the film, then take it out. Your camera is now ready to take a photo.

Take Note of the following

- Ensure the batteries have been inserted before you load the film pack
- Avoid direct sunlight when you are loading the film pack
- You are to use only the FUJIFILM INSTAX mini film and no other.
- When you load the film, never press the two rectangular holes on the back.

- Never open the back cover until you have exhausted the film; else, the rest of the film will be exposed and it will turn to white. And the film can no longer be used.
- Do not use a film pack beyond its shelf life; or else, it may spoil the camera.
- To learn more, check the instructions and warnings on FUJIFILM INSTAX mini film.

3. Taking Pictures

Before you take a photo, you need to know that this camera has what is known as a light-meter, that is a device inside of it that is reading the amount of light that is coming into the camera and it is right at the top of the camera, you will see the two- little dots that's where the light coming in is, so when you are taking photos do not cover these dots with your hand in any way because it will damage every shot you take.

The way this works is that, the camera is looking at the amount of light and deciding what sort of settings it should give you, to get the right brightness of your photo.

All it is doing is that it is putting a little red light on one of the settings and that is how the camera has been configured, you are the one who has to change the setting. You will have to manually adjust the settings but the camera is going to aid you.

So what you need to do, is to look for where that little red light is and you have to turn the dial until the dots lines up with the red light. You have to remember to do that, otherwise, your photos would not come out properly.

Also take note that this camera has what is known as a **minimum focusing distance.** That means a minimum amount of space between the camera and the subject where it can actually get a sharp picture, if you go any closer, it's not going to work. The required distance is 60 centimeters or 24 inches, make sure you don't get closer than that, and ensure you are back a little ways and then you will get sharp, good photos.

Another important thing to note when you are at the minimum focusing distance, is that the framing won't be exactly what you see in the viewfinder, so make sure you give your subject a little extra space, so you don't end up cutting off anything important.

The viewfinder is just at the top left behind the camera, this is what you look through to compose your photo and when you look through it, you will notice that there is a circle in the center of it, that is showing you where the center of your frame is to help you line things up if you want, but it actually becomes more important when we use the close up attachment lens.

Now, the close up attachment lens is in a form of a "white circle" that comes along with the mini 9, this is going to let you shoot at a distance between 35 centimeters and 50 centimeters, so this means you can shoot closer than the default 60 centimeters.

But you have to put the attachment lens in the camera which is quite easy to do, the instruction is to put it while the camera is turned off, but sometimes, when you try it that way it pushes the lens in, so you may want to take the lens and pop it on the lens on the camera and then it comes on.

Why it is important to use this close up attachment lens is that when you look through the viewfinder, you are not going to compose with the whole viewfinder screen, but the circle in the center will now become the top right corner of your frame and you are going to use the bottom left quadrant to compose the photo.

Just take a look through it when you are doing that, the only thing is that you are getting closer than normal, so you have to use less of the viewfinder but practice with it and you will get used to it.

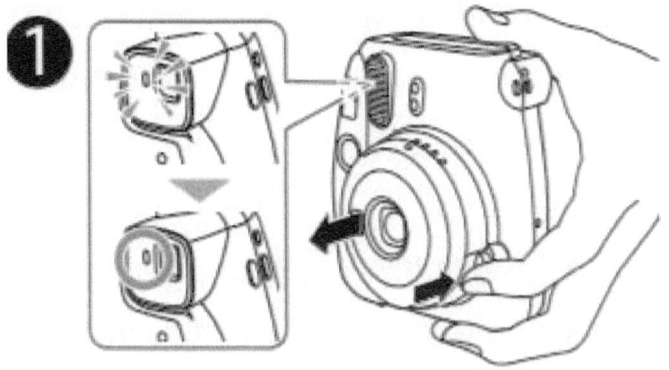

To take a photo, you need to first turn the camera on and this is done by pressing the power button. The flash charging lamp on the left of the eyepiece will start blinking once the camera comes on (this indicates that the flash is charging). Note that you cannot take a photo while the lamp is blinking.

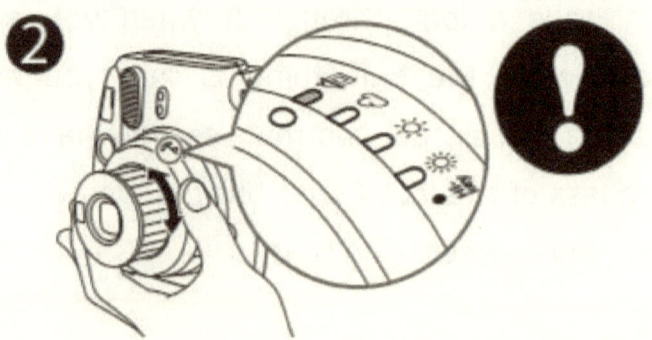

Turn the camera towards the subject, then turn the brightness adjustment dial to move to the position ☀/☁/☼ where the lamp is lit.

The camera has an automatic flash, you can't turn this flash off while you are indoors, and that is really helpful because, it's going to help you see the subject.

The flash has a range of up to 2.7meters, if something is further away from that, the flash would not be able to light them up. Another important tip, especially if you are taking photos of people or something, is that the light from the flash is not too sharp, so you will get better results outdoors.

The light is often softer-it looks better on faces, so I will recommend that if you are taking photos of your loved ones, friends or relatives, try to do that outdoors more and you will like the results

❸ **Vertical image** **Horizontal image**

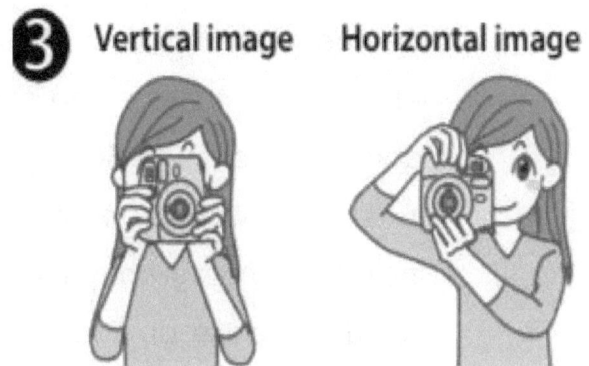

Hold the camera firmly, be sure of the desired composition of the final image, whether it is vertical or horizontal, then press the shutter button.

- Keep a distance from the subject of at least 0.6 m. The flash can reach up to a range of between 0.6 m and 2.7 m to the subject.
- Note that the subject will be out of focus if you are using the regular lens and the distance is less than 0.6 m.

  For short distance photography, use the close-up lens. Using it helps you to capture the subject between 35 cm and 50 cm.
- In short-distance photography (including photography using the provided close-up lens), the centre of the subject in the viewfinder will be on the upper right on the actual print.

Important Tips on Holding the Camera

If the image is horizontal, hold the camera with the flash lampface at the top.

Never take pictures where flash photography is forbidden

Be careful while taking your shots, so that you don't cover the light sensor, flash lampface, flash, lens or film ejection slot with your fingers or with the camera strap.

Never grasp the lens barrel when positioning the camera; else, the finished print may not look as expected.

Look carefully into the view finder and make sure the "O" mark appears in the centre.

Be careful, so you don't touch the lens surface when you press the shutter button.

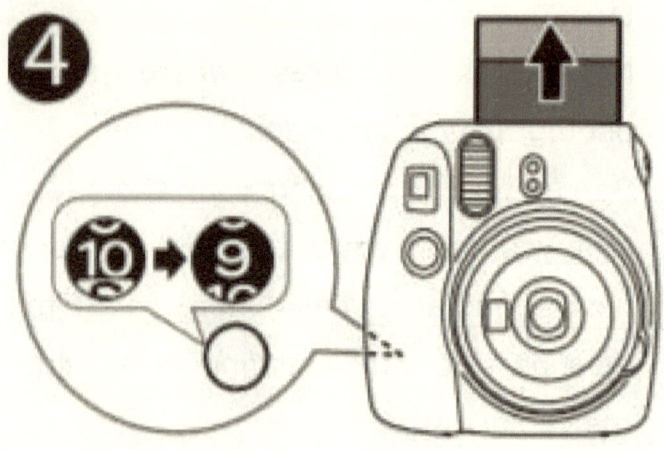

Whenever you take a photo, the number on the film counter will decrease from "10" to display the number of photos left, and "0" is displayed when you have exhausted the film pack.

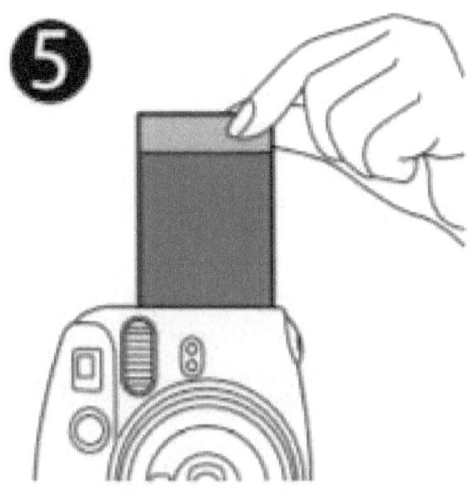

When you have ejected the film, (the camera will stop making sound), carefully hold the edge of the film, and take it out.

The film develops at about 90 seconds, and then you will see the shot you took coming up. Now when you take the photo out, don't shake it. Do not squish it, and do not touch the photo at all, you are to hold it by the edges, or by the bottom.

Note again that these are like complex chemicals, if you are touching or bending it, it's going to get damaged and you will most likely get unpleasant results, something like a thumbprint may appear on your photo or the colours may go really weird especially if you are using this with kids, don't let them get their little fingers on the photos or they may spoil it, so take the photo out carefully and set it down gently, let it develop and then you can look at it.

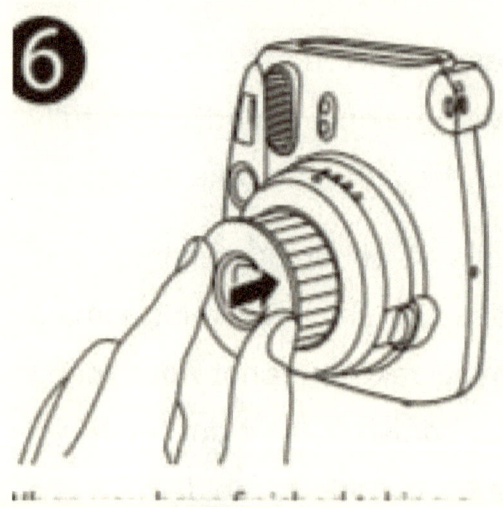

When you have finished taking shots, push the lens barrel to turn the camera off.

CHAPTER 2: Unloading the INSTAX Mini Film Pack

When you see "0" displayed on the film counter, unload the film pack following the procedure below and as stated on the INSTAX mini film pack instructions.

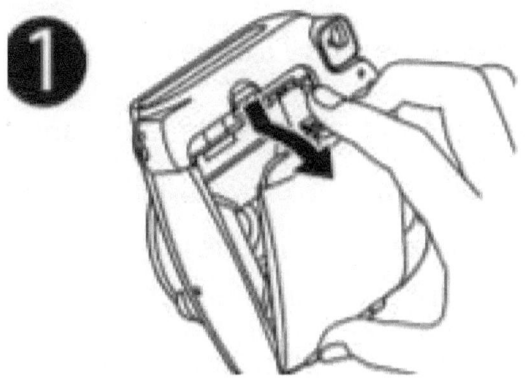

Press down the back cover lock to open the back cover.

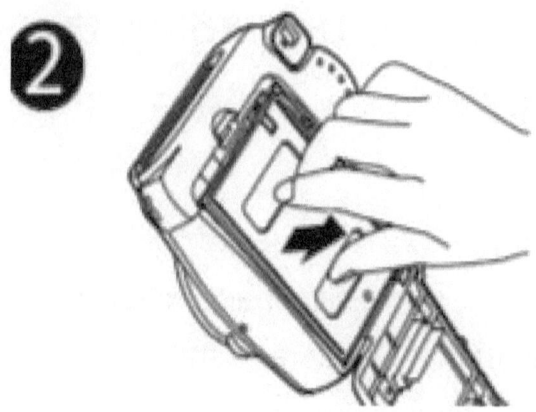

Firmly hold the rectangular holes on the film pack, then pull it out straight

Using the Close-Up Lens (Selfie)

You can take photos of objects close-up and you can also take photos of yourself using the self-portrait mirror (selfie), this is possible because the Fujifilm Instax mini 9 camera has a selfie mirror in-built. You will see a little shiny mirror very close to the camera lens, so that you can take a nice selfie and actually see what is going on. The best thing to use is the close-up attachment lens when taking selfie, otherwise you have to hold it as far away as you can. So use the selfie mirror with the close up attachment lens and you will have satisfying results.

WARNING

- Do not look through the close-up lens at the sun or other strong light. Blindness or vision problems may occur.

Caution

- Do not leave the close-up lens in the places exposed to strong sunlight. Personal injury or fire could result if the lens should accidentally concentrate the sunbeams on an object or a person
- Always switch the camera off the before you attach/detach the close-up lens
- Never turn the close-up lens when you attach/detach it; otherwise, the tabs

at the back of the camera may get
broken.

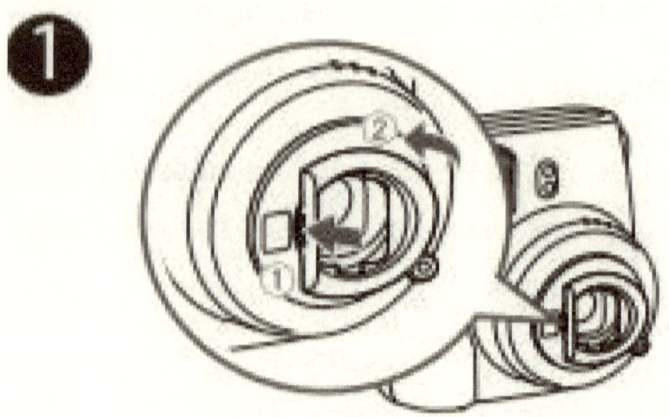

Attach the left tab on the back to the left of
the lens (1), then attach the right tab (2) so
that it clicks into place.

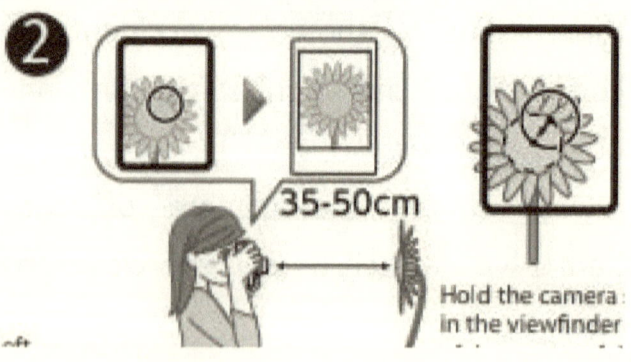

35-50cm

Hold the camera
in the viewfinder

Hold the camera in a way that the "O" mark in the viewfinder is on the upper right of the center of the subject (see the illustration above) then take a photo.

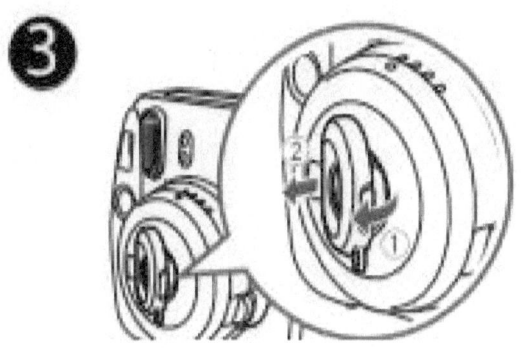

Lift up the right side of the close-up lens supporting the left side, (1) then detach it (2)

Chapter 3: TAKING SELFIE-PORTRAITS

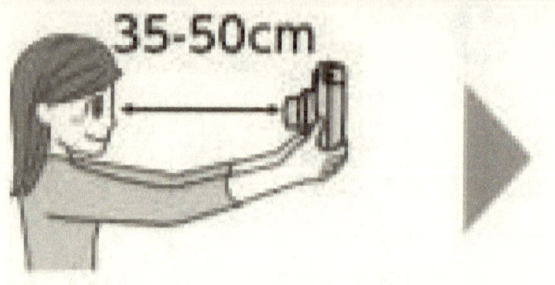

Hold the camera firmly and carefully, and keep a distance of 35 cm to 50 cm between you and the edge of the lens

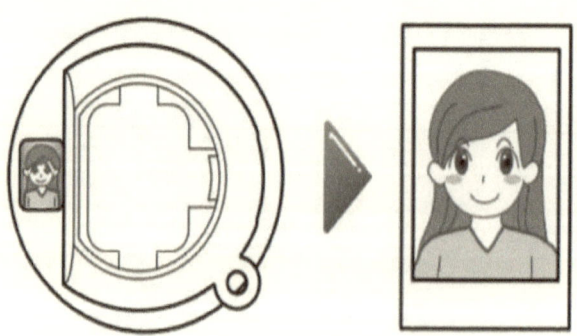

Use the self-portrait mirror to confirm the composition, then take a photo

IMPORTANT Keys on taking a lighter (Hi-Key) picture

If you are new to the Instax mini 9 camera, you will see the light meter-like a little dot with other little dots on the top of the camera lens.

You will see the image of a house on one of the dots indicating it's for taking photos indoor, a cloud image for cloudish setting situations outside, there is a sun image for bright weather and full sun image for really bright weather.

So don't make your decisions based on the weather around you again, use the light meter, and that will help you get the right exposure.

The last dot like button is the High-key which is going to make the photo brighter than the camera thinks it should be.

The manual states that you shouldn't use this high-key outdoors, because it's going to make things way too bright, so you should probably experiment with that more indoors, but it would be fun to look at, so give it a trial.

One of the really interesting things about photos taken with the Fujifilm Instax mini 9 camera, is that you can label the bottom with a pen to remember what was going on in the photo or write a little nice note, for someone or something like that, so make sure you do that every once in a while just for fun.

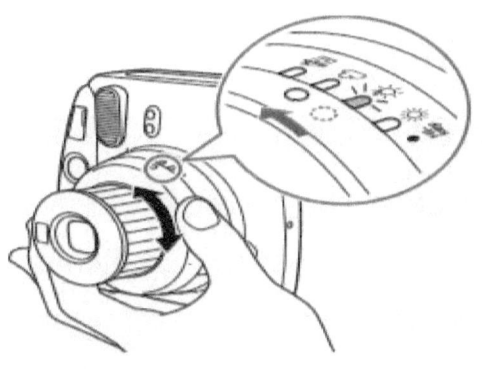

Position at which the lamp lights	☀	☀	☁	🏠
Position to set the dial for a lighter (Hi key picture	☀	☁	🏠	**Hi-Key**

To take a lighter (Hi-key) picture, set the position of the brightness adjustment dial to the position of the mode darker than the mode for which the lamp on the dial lights (as shown in the image above)

CHAPTER 4: TROUBLE SHOOTING OPTIONS

During operation some problems may occur some of these problems are highlighted below:

A. Problems

- If the shutter release doesn't trip

Possible causes of this problem may be:

1. That the battery power is low
2. Or the batteries are not loaded correctly
3. Also maybe Power is not turned on
4. And if the camera has remained unused for roughly 5minutes while the power turned on

Recommended Solutions

1. Replace the batteries with new ones
2. Make sure you load the batteries correctly

3. Firmly press the power button to turn on power, and release your hand once the camera is on.

4. Press the power button after retracting the lens or press the shutter release button to restore the power on state

B. Problems

- When you see the lamp on the view finder blinking and the shutter release doesn't trip

Possible causes

- It's possible the Flash is charging

Recommended Solutions

- Ensure to wait until the lamp on the brightness adjustment dial is lit without blinking

C. Problems

- If the film pack won't load into your camera, or fails to load into your camera smoothly.

The Possible causes may be:

1. That the film pack is not for your camera type
2. Or you are not loading the film pack correctly

Recommended Solutions

1. Use FUJIFILM INSTAX mini film only. (No other films can be used)
2. Align the yellow line on the film pack with the yellow positioning mark in your camera. Make sure you follow the INSTAX mini film pack instructions.

D. Problems

If all the lamps on the brightness adjustment dial blink at the same time.

The possible causes are:

1. The battery power is low and it takes a long time to charge the flash
2. Perhaps a more serious issue with your camera has occurred

Recommended Solutions

Replace the batteries with new ones while the power is turned on (when the lens is extended)

IMPORTANT NOTICE:

- Replace the batteries only when the power is turned on. If you replace the batteries while the power is turned off (when the lens is retracted), the lamps on the brightness adjustment dial blink after turning the power even with new batteries.

- When the problem is due to reason (1), the lamps on the brightness adjustment dial will turn off after replacing the batteries.

- If the problem is due to reason (2), the lamps on the brightness adjustment dial will blink even after replacing the batteries. In this case, turn off the power and remove the batteries immediately, then contact an authorized FUJIFILM repair center.

E. Problems

- The red lamp on the view finder lights up

Possible causes can be:

- Maybe the battery power is low

Recommended Solutions

- Replace the batteries with new ones

PRINTED PICTURES

Some problems may occur after the photo has been shot and the picture is printed, some of these problems are enumerated below:

F. Problems

- The finished print looks over exposed (white in colour)

Possible causes are:

1. The method you used in measuring the subject brightness is unsuitable
2. If the brightness adjustment dial setting is incorrect
3. If the ambient temperature is low (below $+5^0C/+41^0F$)
4. Or if the background is too dark in comparison with the subject.
5. And if the light sensor or flash sensor window is blocked

Recommended Solutions

1. Point the lens towards the center of the subject and measure the subject brightness

2. While pointing the lens toward the subject, turn the brightness adjustment dial to set the brightness to that for which the lamp lights

3. Before you start taking pictures, put your camera in a warm place to bring it to room temperature.

4. Turn the brightness dial one step toward the ☀ (light) direction

5. When you are taking pictures, be careful not to cover the two small windows next to the flash on the camera.

G. Problems

- The finished print looks under exposed (Dark)

Possible causes includes

1. The method used in measuring the brightness of the subject is unsuitable
2. If the brightness adjustment dial setting is not correct
3. If the ambient temperature is high (above $+40^0C/+104^0F$).
4. Also if the picture was taken with direct light in front of you
5. In cases where the flash lampface was blocked
6. Or if the background is too bright in comparison with the subject.
7. Also if the flash did not reach the subject.
8. If the flash reflected back from a mirror or window glass
9. If grasping the lens barrel did not allow the shutter to work properly.

The recommended solutions are as follows:

1. Point the lens toward the center of the subject and measure the subject brightness.
2. While pointing the lens toward the subject, turn the brightness adjustment dial to set the brightness to that for which the brightness adjustment dial lamp lights.
3. Before you start taking pictures, place your camera in a cool place. When the picture comes out from your camera, keep it away from places or objects with excessively high temperature.
4. Take a picture with the light behind you, or turn the brightness adjustment dial one step toward the 🏠 direction.
5. When holding your camera, be careful not to block the flash lampface with your finger or strap.

6. Turn the brightness adjustment dial one step toward the 🏠 direction

7. You should be within 0.6 m to 2.7 m from the subject before you take a shot

8. Adjust your position when taking the picture away from the mirror or window glass

9. Do not grasp the lens barrel when you take pictures.

H. Problems

- The picture is out of focus

Possible causes include:

1. Perhaps the shooting range is too close to the subject

2. Or maybe the lens is not clean

3. Or your camera was shaken while you were taking pictures

Recommended solutions

1. Always clean the lens
2. Take pictures with a distance of at least 0.6 m between you and your subject
3. Firmly hold your camera and press the shutter release button carefully.

I. Problems

- The picture is blurred

Possible causes may be that the:

1. Picture was not permitted to develop without touching, and pressure was being applied or other interface immediately it got ejected from the camera
2. The picture did not come out smoothly

Recommended Solutions

1. Do not block the film exit with your finger

2. Do not press onto or fold the picture

J. Problems

- The subject in the viewfinder has shifted in finished print.

The Possible cause for this problem may be:

- That the shooting range is too close to the subject.

Recommended Solutions

You should take your pictures with a distance of at least 0.6 m between you and your subject.

Chapter 5: HOW TO CARE FOR YOUR CAMERA

There are some common ways for you to take proper care of your camera, they are as follows:

1. If you are not using your camera for a long a period of time, unload the batteries and keep it safe from heat, dust and moisture.

2. Your camera is a precision instrument. So do not let it get wet and do not expose to sand.

3. Do not use a strap made for cellular phones or other similar electronic products. Most of these straps are always too weak to hold your camera securely. For safety purpose, use only straps designed for your camera and use it only as specifically intended and instructed.

4. Do not use solvent such as thinner and alcohol to remove soil from your camera.

5. Use an air blower to remove soil and dust from the lens, viewfinder windows e.t.c and by wiping lightly with a piece of soft cloth.

6. Always keep the film chamber and camera interior clean to avoid damaging the films.

7. In case of hot weather, don't leave your camera in a closed car or on the beach, and do not leave it in moist places.

8. Moth repellant gas such as naphthalene can negatively affect your camera and films. So avoid keeping your camera or films in a chest with mothballs

9. Note that your camera is computer-controlled. So in case you experience

an operational issue, remove the batteries and then reload them.

10.   Note also that the temperature range within which your camera can be used is $+5^0C/+41^0F$ to $+40^0C/+104^0F$

Chapter 6: HOW TO CARE FOR YOUR INSTAX mini FILM AND PRINT

Check the FUJIFILM INSTAX mini film for film use instructions. Follow all instructions for safe and proper use. Below are a ways you can care for your Instax mini 9 camera

1. Keep the film in a cool and dry place. Do not leave the film in a place where the temperature is extremely high (e.g in a closed car)

2. Once you load a film pack, use the film as soon as possible.

3. If the film has been kept in a place where the temperature is extremely high or low, bring it to room temperature before starting to take pictures

4. Make sure you use the film before the expiration or 'Use Before' date.

5. You should prevent your camera from airport checked luggage inspection and other strong X-ray illumination. The effect of fogging, e.t.c may appear on your unused film. So it is recommended that you carry the camera and/or the film onto the aircraft as carry-on luggage (check with each airportds for more information).

6. Always avoid strong light, keep the developed prints in a cool and dry place.

7. Do not puncture, tear or cut the INSTAX mini film. If the film becomes damaged, do not use it again.

To know more on how to handle the film and prints, check the instructions and warnings on the FUJIFILM INSTAX mini film.

CONCLUSION

Keep these photos safe and a good way to do that is by getting a very good album. You can also get cool lenses that snap on to the front that will put different color filters on your camera.

So that could be an interesting experiment for you, you can also get cases for your camera too, there are different types of Instax mini film, there are colored and black and white film, depending on which you want.

You need the Fujifilm Instax mini 9 camera especially if you go on a lot of trips, and even if you don't go on a lot of trips, you still need the Fujifilm Instax mini 9 to capture beautiful images, and keep good memories of places, stories and events.